THE BITTER SWEET LOVE
of Randolph K. McKinnon

A Poetry Sequence
From John Makinson

First published 2020 by IRON Press
5 Marden Terrace
Cullercoats
North Shields
NE30 4PD
tel +44(0)191 2531901
ironpress@xlnmail.com
www.ironpress.co.uk

ISBN 978-1-9997636-7-1
Printed by Imprint Digital

© The poems, the author 2020
© This collection, IRON Press 2020

Cover and book design, Brian Grogan and Peter Mortimer

Typeset in Georgia 10pt

IRON Press books are distributed by
NBN International
and represented by Inpress Ltd
Milburn House, Dean Street
Newcastle upon Tyne NE1 1LF
tel: +44(0)191 2308104
www.inpressbooks.co.uk

Wanting is lust
Needing is love

Modus Operandi

I BEGAN THIS SEQUENCE OF POEMS IN THE NINETEEN EIGHTIES, AND IT WAS with the intention of writing a fictional love story in poetic form. However, after I'd written eight or nine of them, I began to realise that a traditional story of lost love or love betrayed followed by lovelorn anguish didn't offer anything new. So I put them in a folder, thinking I might use them if I eventually came up with a suitable or, more accurately, unusual story line, though I couldn't help thinking that what seemed more probable was that they'd end up being incorporated into another collection. Either way, they lay in the folder for several years.

It was only when I began to digest a story I'd read in a newspaper that I realised I'd found what I was looking for. It was one of those 'it could only happen in America' stories, and was about a woman – a wife and mother – who'd sued a hospital where she'd been advised to have a hysterectomy as a cure for severe period pains. Before the operation she had been a devoted wife, but after it, so the court was told, she had become hugely unfaithful to the husband, who eventually divorced her.

Her case was that she had received bad advice from the hospital, and as a result, she had lost the husband she loved. Her lawyer called a psychiatrist to the stand to testify that her infidelities were a subconscious compensation for her no longer being able to bear children.

The story struck a chord with me because some years earlier my first wife and I had been friendly with a couple whose own story was not dissimilar. In their case, the woman discovered she could never have children, and soon after was having affairs with several men. Their relationship, too, ended in divorce.

The psychology therefore didn't seem too far-fetched, and, if I remember rightly, the court thought so, too, because they awarded her two million dollars in compensation. Nice work if you can get it!

So, with a little adaptation, I had my story line. Of course, when you start writing something – and in particular poetry – it often leads you into unexpected areas. I came to think that my two characters were truly in love and would not leave the relationship whatever the provocation. This, however, presented me with a problem. If I pursued this line of thinking, it would leave me with no ending, or one that was weak, and as I wanted the ending to have some poignancy, I chose to have the woman die of cancer. I could not have imagined it was to become far more poignant than I could ever have foreseen.

All writers inevitably bring something of their own lives to their work, so whilst the story is fictional, it does have some autobiographical features – though, apart from the title, I will leave it to the reader to imagine which ones those might be!

The working title of the collection underwent at least a dozen changes before I arrived at the final one. If circumstances had been different, Randolph K. Mckinnon could have been my own name. My mother thought of naming me Randolph Kennerley after her father, but eventually thought better of it. And my surname was Anglicized from McKinnon when my ancestors arrived in Lancashire from Scotland in the Nineteenth Century.

For Hazel and Jeff, Paul, Karen, Angie, and Jayne.

John Makinson

The Poems

Winter Honeymoon in the Cotswolds	9
Nest Building	10
The Tamarind Tree	11
Crime and Punishment	12
Do I Dare Disturb a Peach	13
Paris	15
Quid Pro Quo	16
In Vino Veritas	17
Ivan	18
Line Dancing	19
Rome: In Santa Maria della Vittoria	20
Anus Horibilis	21
Crows Feeding	22
Llandudno	26
Warnings	28
Non Sequitur	29
Victrix Ludorum	30
The Tale of the Rampant Rabbit	32
Two's Company	33
As If	34

Cunnilingus	35
Her Definitions	36
Cogito Ergo Piss	37
Vidi, Vici, Veni	38
Lex Talionis	39
Amsterdam: Caveat Emptor	40
New York, New York	42
Capricorn	44
Her Answer	46
Her Story: No Fairy Tale	47
Carnation	49
Ghosts	51
This Will be It from Now on, I Suppose	52
If I Could Write You a Letter, My Love	53
Starling	55

Remainders:

Anniversaries	57
Raindrops	58
Arsy Versy	59
Four Seasons of a Bad Year	60

Winter honeymoon in the Cotswolds

On the fourth day it snowed.
Wrapped in our sheet, we watched it falling,
gently, gently,
caressing the ground.
How unlike rain, you said.
By afternoon the world was white,
but the room was a nest
and silent with our whispered love,
the bed a delight.
Oh! We were lost in gentleness.
We did not think that skies could crash,
that rooms weren't always warm.

Nest Building

Out buying bedding, we left the store
and laughed as we squeezed through the door.
Each carrying a pillow, plump and light,
we crossed the square in great delight.
I can't recall whose blow struck first,
but the splendour of the moment burst
like a champagne cork. And, oh, what bliss!
Each clout was like the sweetest kiss.
They stared at us as if we were mad
or jealous, perhaps, at the laughter we had.

The Tamarind Tree

We sat by the Med.
I remember your smile as we broke the bread.
The wine was red,
and we sipped, you and me.
We sipped it beneath a tamarind tree.

The moon came bright
as evening descended into night.
A man lit a light,
and we kissed, you and me.
We kissed beneath the tamarind tree.

The air was still.
The waiter came and we ate our fill.
He put down the bill,
and we laughed, you and me,
as we talked beneath the tamarind tree.

Intent on staying,
I can't recall what we were saying,
but guitars were playing.
We danced, you and me.
We danced beneath the tamarind tree.

Crime and Punishment

You broke the vase my parents
bought.
I came home from work
and found you contrite.
Accidents happen, as well I knew,
but I made my face stern
to see what advantage might accrue.

It was a Thursday: the night
we did our weekly shop.

In our bedroom,
I made you put on your shortest skirt:
"Now take off your knickers!"
You giggled at the pleasure
or the punishment you perceived,
till I jingled my keys
and said, "Let's go."

I found it revealing, shall we say,
watching you get things
from the bottom shelf.
Alas, it wasn't a busy night!

When we got home,
we didn't unpack
until we'd had the most frenzied sex.

And I think you deliberately broke
the chair,
the clock,
the mirror ....

Do I Dare Disturb a Peach

The room is warm, and the unlined curtains
gauze the sunlight of late afternoon.
A strip of dazzling light picks dust motes
as it falls across your nakedness.
Across one buttock and your lower back
it moves inexorably, unrushed towards
your slightly parted legs, as if
to guide me, like Macbeth's dagger,
to some consummate fate.
Even before the light can reach,
you are showing that sweetest,
pornographic part of you, already moistened,
I suspect, by that self-indulgent,
pre-sleep ritual you enjoy so much.

Should I play the voyeur, for my own sake?
Should I watch or should I wake?

Postponing the moment, I stop the player
that's softly singing
that country and western stuff you like
and look for something more appropriate
for what we need. I find a Puccini,
remembering how you climaxed once
to *Un Bel Di* in a room
full of candles, champagne, and love.
I click to *E Lucevan le Stelle*,
adjust the sound and let it swell,
as I focus on your pornographic parts,
half hoping it might make you stir.

Should I play the voyeur, for my own sake?
Should I watch or should I wake?

I know you would not be annoyed,
would smile, say something rude,
hold me gently, close your eyes again
and part your lips slightly for a kiss.
I know you would not be annoyed,
would smile, and close your eyes again
for the waking and the taking and the aching,
for the teasing and the easing and the pleasing.
And yet I hold back still, paralysed,
feeling unmanned by indecision,
wondering should I take off all my clothes
for the waking and the taking and the aching,
stand there undignified some moments
before the teasing and the easing and the pleasing.
And should I play the voyeur, for my own sake?
Should I watch or should I take?
Should I disturb the kitten as it sleeps,
to stroke its fur and make it purr
for my own sake?

Paris

We'd jostled with crowds before
Notre Dame and The Eiffel Tower
and taken a batteau along the Seine
on a perfect April day.

Later we found a quiet café.
We talked as if we owned the world.
You spoke about living there someday.
'You'd be my Henry Miller,' you said,
'I'd be your Anais Nin.'

I smiled at the thought,
though I knew you meant it.

That evening we ate Vietnamese,
and you laughed each time
I tried to speak French.

Walking back at a gentle pace,
through an open window on the second floor,
we heard a woman being pleasured –
no fake, for sure!

We grinned at each other.
You pulled my arm,
and we quickened our steps
in Paris.

Quid Pro Quo

We played the game where we tossed a coin
for who'd be the master and who the slave.
You thought I cheated the first few times
because I won.

My imagination
ran to nothing more than sex.

I used a hairbrush on your bare arse.

You went the whole way:
wore shiny boots and acquired a cane,
had me do the shopping, clean the house.
And woe betide if I got it wrong.

Afterwards,
sometimes with my arse on fire,
we'd roger each other half to death
all night.

In Vino Veritas

Lying in bed on a cold afternoon –
the bed was warm,
the wine had gone,
already we'd made love –
when you said,
"Who do you fancy of our friends?"

I suspected a trap, but falling
into it nevertheless,
I mentioned a name.

"Oh, so do I!" you instantly said.
And with so much glee, it gave me a shock.
The possibilities
raced round my head,
and when we made love
a few minutes later,
we both came hard.
You never spoke of it afterwards.
And now it will not leave my head.
I think of it always when we're in bed.

Ivan

Sits on the sill stock still
unaware his tail's a law unto itself,
watching a bird pecking its way
across the lawn. Says
*I'd show you a thing or two
if it weren't for this glass.*

Jumps on the sofa
where we lounge and rubs
his head against your chin.
Will find the spot and scrunch
into a throbbing ball, saying
I'm a part of this family too.

Comes round our legs
and lets his tail linger against
your calf. Sometimes opens his mouth
in a silent miaow. Says
I can do things you don't understand.

Jumps on the bed
while we make love, and watches
with his head aslant. And
(with his knackers removed) says
*This looks jolly interesting
whatever it is!*

Line Dancing

Suede and tassels, leather boots
and cowboy hat:
you say it makes you horny.

When you come home
your thong gets whizzed.

Grabbing the iron bed frame
with both hands
you ride me like you'd ride a horse,
your tassels flicking madly.

It's another way you've found
to thrill me.

(Thank God you haven't any spurs,
or I think you'd bloody kill me!)

Rome: In Santa Maria della Vittoria

The road eventually led us there.
It looked like a disused cinema
and took an age to find. We avoided,
the discomfort of the beggar's eyes
waiting to waylay us
at the shabby door.

Inside was all magnificence.
The crowd was all around
the Bernini piece
and more jovial
than anywhere we'd been that day.

It was smaller than I'd imagined,
but dazzling, nonetheless, and rare.
The crowd had me shifting
from place to place
for the optimum angle to take a shot.

With you at my side I wondered if
I could discretely use my hand
to fetch you off, and add it
to our list of 'done it there'.
Standing in front of such a fuse
of religion, art, erotica
it scarcely seemed profane.

Your eyes met mine and knew.
"You dirty devil!" you mouthed
at me. "You would an' all!"

Anus Horibilis

I remember the first time we did it
like that.
You were up for it more than I,
being frightened of hurting you,
though you kept saying
It's okay,
It's okay.

You came several times,
to my surprise, but said
it was different though, more deep,
more subtle than the usual way.

Afterwards you asked me if
I'd ever
fancied doing it
with
a guy.

How could you ask me something
like that!

No! Never!
Not in a thousand years!

Crows Feeding

i. Words

An old man should have stumbled
drunkenly in front of us,
cursing and hawking, haunting us
with his rancid camel's breath;

or a woman, harassed beyond wit
by several brats and a stupid pram,
should have lashed out her hand,
using such language as destroys all hope.

But I remember instead how you
fumbled for change
till you found enough to park our car
and the almost tears you had in your eyes.

The sky should have bounced the pavement
with its fiercest rain or hail,
or ice should have scrunched
beneath our tentative footstepped way.

A bitter wind should have pierced our clothes,
but the day was warm and gentle,
and I think the flowers in wooden boxes
in the square were at their best.

Inside the waiting room you tapped
your cigarettes. I tried to hold your hand
yet offered no words to break
the heartbeat silence of the room.

You turned several times to look at the door,
as if it were the courtroom of our lives,
before tossing the packet
still unopened back in your bag.

We knew the worst before she spoke.
Her voice was sympathetically soft
but the words gavel hard
and the verdict offered no reprieve.

Phrases fell like bombs from a B52.
'This isn't a choice.' She shook her head.
You squeezed my hand when that awful word
'Removed' exploded in our brains.

It was the only time I've seen you cretinous.
The doctor merely shook her head
then spoke of several weeks off work.
You wanted to know about scars.

ii. Silence

I couldn't wait to be out of there
and home. Except it was worse:
a counting house of silence, silence.
Silence like the roar of a shell.

We mainly contemplate our future joys.
We can't take in such days as these, and silence –
where silence should not be – unnerves
as much as any midnight scream.

All I could think of was to make
some tea, handling the mugs in the kitchen
as if they were precious, and the kettle,
like a klaxon, made me wince.

You took the mug without a word,
without a look. You'd lit another cigarette;
I sat and watched as you exhaled the smoke;
I watched the smoke become a nothingness.

So far away you were, sitting there
across the room. And I, like a coward,
grateful in a way. Grateful that you didn't let
your eyes meet mine. I also needed time.

Time. Like a white swan, it glides through
our lives. And all its trivial moments
which compose an adagio of our days, patter
pianissimo, almost unnoticed, until we die.

But this was a day when the fat,
black crows crept stealthily, unbidden
and unannounced into our lives to steal
our looked for harvest home of happiness.

We seldom get the payoff we desire.
The folly of life's blueprints ridicule
our days, reducing them to nothing more
than the spawn and bone of a random universe.

And all the while this universe expands
until we wonder where our lives
will end it all. I only know
we will not add to it, you and I.

You didn't drink the tea I made. Several times
I left the room – to return the mug – to make
another – to go to the toilet, where
I did the codebreaker in the daily rag.

Eventually, I asked you if you wanted
anything to eat. You shook your head.
"I'd have made a good mother," you said.
then sobbed great sobs into your hands.

iii. Healing

We returned to the trivial bit by bit,
found things to occupy our time,
said we might go away before the op –
people at work would understand.

We talked about my friends, about yours.
We stayed up late, avoiding that room
and its burnt-out altar of procreation,
willing each other to make the first move.

Even then, we laid there in the silent night.
I searched for your hand and held it
awhile and wished we could be spoons
your warm and gentle breath against my neck.

"Do it to me." Like a thunderbolt: you
didn't even move your head. And I
made love to you as you laid there
and clung to me as if I were a god.

Llandudno

I remember
how the wind blew an edge
from the Irish Sea,
how we sat and ate sandwiches from *Marks*,
the book you bought but didn't read,
the sound of the sea
on the rocks by the pier,

and a moment
on a flag flying turret
of Conwy Castle,
the wind gently tugging
the hair away from your sad face.

The place we stayed was stuffed
with laughter and wartime songs:
a happy breed, reliving the past
and supping the last
few drops from life.

One evening we stayed with them –
by accident, I rather think.
You laughed that night,
with a drink or two inside you,
and joined in the songs from –
jolly, now – remembered wars.

Those ancient men,
they couldn't take
their twinkling eyes away from you,
a real life Jane
with stockinged legs
and a fabulous chest.

You pinched a cap and sat
on several jolly laps.
The women didn't seem to mind.
for you were a superstar,
way,
way out
of their husbands' league.

The following day you joked with me,
"Perhaps we'll be able to stay 5 star
without any kids!"

Warnings

i.

You like to flirt with danger;
live life while you can.
We went hot-air-ballooning,
and you flirted with the man.

ii.

We booked for *The Rocky Horror Show,*
but I went down with flu.
In sussies and a see-through dress
you went with your mate Stu.

iii.

You danced with a guy you knew from work;
his hand was up your dress.
You called him a dirty bugger,
but you giggled nonetheless.

Non Sequitur

Then one night you came home late.
I asked you where you'd been.
I said,
"I asked you where you'd been!"
You said,
"I've been to London to visit The Queen!"

I watched you from the bathroom door;
I watched you pat your hair.
I asked,
"So how were Sue and Claire?"
You turned.
"Oh pass me a towel – they're on the chair."

And then in bed you turned your back
and didn't want my love.
I asked you,
"Don't you want some love?"
You said,
"Oh, go to sleep, my turtle dove!"

Victrix Ludorum

You said it would do us both some good,
that the others' husbands were fine with it,
I could play some golf
and try to drink myself to death
with the rest of my mates,
so I agreed.

When you got back, we went at it
like ferrets on viagara.
But I have my sources.
I later found out about what went on.

When challenged you
didn't even deny it –

All of us got carried away
and
They meant nothing.

They!
They!

It's you I love.

Your system of points
would have made a mathematician proud:
points for each guy, points for each time,
points for oral, points for length.

And a bottle of Bolli for the one with the
most.
You were all very busy
by the look of the scores:
looks like
you all got plenty
of 'it'.

All I got was eighteen holes
and a share in a bottle of decent champagne.

The Tale of the Rampant Rabbit

You give them all names –
male of course.
So much better than *G-spot Vibe*
or *Rambo De-luxe*,
more personal.

It never bothered me at all,
especially as I often gave you
a buzzing time.
(Though the *Jelly Green Giant* –
which you described as 'gelatinous' –
pricked my ego just a tad).

But she – and she kept the name
with which she was christened –
was another tale.

I'd thought you were insatiable
till you brought her home.

Your glee was all too obvious.
You went through her various attributes,
holding her against your nose,
as you were told by Claire.
"It does the lot!" you cheerily said.

You disappeared to our bedroom,
and I didn't see you again that night.

Sometimes you have to act!

I shall disembowel her,
draw out her guts,
cut off her ears,
and be damned with the R.S.P.C.V.

Two's Company

You suggested we tried
a threesome;
said you had a friend at work
who was really keen.

I thought all my birthdays
had come in one go,
till I opened the door
and there stood Joe.

As if

I shop for food and cook the meals,
your mother does the dusting,
if it wasn't for me, the garden tools
would be in the shed and rusting.
When you undress, you scatter clothes;
I find them where they fall.
I've had enough of your slatternly ways;
it will not do at all.

You certainly like your beauty sleep;
it's noon before you rise,
then take an age to do your hair
and put make-up on your eyes.
You spend a fortune on your clothes;
from store to shop you trawl.
Okay you look terrific,
but it will not do at all.

When I complain, you hug my neck,
you smile and play like cupid.
As if I'd fall for such soft-soap!
Oh, you must think I'm stupid!
Your clothes come off with a sexy strip.
You'd make an angel fall.
You know the moves to tease a man,
but it will not do at all.

In bed we get athletic,
have marathons of sex.
You joke 'it keeps us bloody fit'
(and it's given me nice pecs).
But it will not do, it will not do,
it will not do at all.
If it wasn't for sex (and my beautiful pecs)
it would not do at all.

Cunnilingus

You no longer mention the new guy
at work. You now wear stockings
instead of tights. And I caught you donning
a brand-spanking-new, expensive thong.
So many times I've held my tongue.

Removing your vest, your bra
can't hide the fading love-bite
on your breast. You realise and cover yourself
by singing the words of some old song.
So many times I've held my tongue.

In the bedroom, after you've gone
out with friends. Discarded garments,
drawers half closed, and the smell of perfume,
persistent and invasively strong.
So many times I've held my tongue.

You have me shave you – there.
Your fingers and your eyes delight, until
I remove your hand and lick its smoothness,
parting your labia with my tongue.
So many times I've used my tongue.

You say you love me - if I say it first -
as if I should be grateful you're still here.
Though we still make love, or have sex,
often, tempestuous, hard and strong.
So many times I've held my tongue.

Her Definitions

One night Stands:

Are someone else's puppy.
It jumps up at you, demands
your attention.
You pick it up and it licks your nose
and amuses you
for a very short while.
But you don't have the barking,
the hairs, the pissing,
the shitting, the smell.
Only its cuteness is a consideration.

Flings:

Are a railway journey.
It can be Trans-Siberian,
Orient Express,
or North Yorkshire Moors.
With any luck you'll be pulled
by steam - huge pistons,
and plenty of sweating
and huffing and puffing
along the way.
But always it has a beginning
and always an end.

Affairs:

Centuries past
it was called bewitchment;
you were tied to a stake;
you were done to death.
Now it's no more than a candle flame.
You put your fingers closer and closer
and hope you don't get burned.

Cogito Ergo Piss

The end of a hot and sweaty August day
now painted on a sky of salmon pink.
How I love these summer evenings
when it's never less than cool
and never more than warm,
the garden rich and living
in the still and perfumed air.
My dahlias are at their peak,
bright yellow, bronze, vermilion.
Each a delight. Your fuchsias, too,
are at their best, deeply, deeply pink
and white. I think of how I make
the joke – *Who fucksia, baby?*
with a hand on your bum –
when I see you bending over them,
lifting a bell and breathing in.
And I wonder how it can be
you love these drooping heads –
red-hot pokers more your style!
On an impulse, I rise from my chair,
open my flies and water the blue
hydrangea that you love.

Vidi, Vici, Veni

I hadn't fancied it one little bit:
a two-day course was not my kind of fun, I must admit.
but she moved her coat so I could sit
                    beside her.

That evening we went out to try the bars.
I may have talked about my wife between the jars;
she said her husband sold used cars
                    to unsuspecting mugs.

She laughed each time I made a joke.
Her eyes met mine each time she sipped her rum and coke.
I liked the way she blew the smoke
                    from her cigarette.

Eventually, a barman rang a bell.
We both got up and must have thought *Oh, What the Hell!*
All the details I need not tell;
                    I'm sure you'll guess.

We used the night until we were both spent.
I'd had a rough two weeks and thought her Heaven sent.
But with the morning light we kissed and went
                    our separate ways.

Lex Talionis

An evening of a day of hard, persistent rain.
You've always loved it, standing in the after-storm,
out in the garden, clutching your mug of tea.
Oh, how I'd love for you to clutch at me
                instead.

Perhaps it reminds you of those moments when
(please excuse me for being crude)
a lover of yours has finished the job,
you smoking, and he lying there with his knob
                all shrunk.

Does he come at you all huge and fierce,
tearing your passion from you in wave after wave.
I wish I were a lion – rampant – or a unicorn,
pawing at the naked ground, my great horn
                gleaming.

More of a beast, I'd have taken a crop
to your upturned arse a long time ago.
In my fantasies you say you were due it,
and afterwards, oh, how you'd beg me to do it
                to you.

What frauds we've become:
you with your lovers and I with my dreams.
I retaliate with a fistful of women,
and we'll carry on swimming
                in our whirlpool of sex.

Amsterdam: Caveat Emptor

We did the usual things:
canal boat ride by evening's lights,
the tulip fields,
Rembrandt's house,
the high life
and the night-life
and the red light.

You wanted to know
if they turned me on,
if I fancied them.
"Oh, no," I said.
"You're all I need."

But you wouldn't give up.
You could always spot my economies.
"What are you scared of?"
'The clap!' I said,
which made you laugh.

You dared me,
said you'd pay
"It can be my treat."

You were serious.

So I went –
predictably for a suspender-clad.

Afterwards
you had to know
the whole fucking lot.
And then you asked me how much it cost.

"How much!
Bloody Hell!" you said.
"I think I'll take it up myself!"

Back at our hotel
we had a session on the bed –
but not before
you'd made me take a shower.

New York, New York

Coming in from Newark
past rundown tenements, the same
squalor we'd left behind,
and uncountable cars
on a New Jersey Turnpike,

emerging into dazzle
from the Lincoln Tunnel
and a first sight – a street
of peepshows and dirty mags
and one vast traffic snarl,
honking like puffins fighting
for their bit of ground.

But you loved each goddam minute
and New York loved you.
Within three days
you were 'How you doin'' it
like a native child.

We rode a carriage
in Central Park.
You had the driver stop
so we could ride the carousel.

The ritual we played
with waiters' tips – you'd slap
away my hand and say,
"Now don't be mean!" then pluck
another dollar from my wad –
was all a piece of it.

Black-marbled Bloomingdales
blew your mind and your salary
for a couple of months –
and had me craving
the pound-shops of home.

And as if Broadway were paved
with gold, we paid way over odds
to see two shows.

So this was New York!
New York! – so good
we fucked like crazy twice
each night
and most mornings too.

Capricorn

It was a different waiting room,
a different door, a different doctor, though
his manner and the atmosphere
were just the same. He bade us sit down.

You'd sat me down two nights before
to tell me what they'd found. You said
it was inoperable. I didn't believe,
or couldn't believe. It was all too much.

He took us through it. Everything
you might expect. And all the time
the three of us dreading an answer
to that awful, 'How long?' question.

And when at last the denouement came,
you didn't flinch. You squeezed my hand
so loud it hurt. "Be brave, my love,"
it said to me. "I need you now."

He started to talk about chemo, but you
cut him short. His eyebrows raised, his mouth
went wide when you told him that
you didn't want it. You'd made up your mind.

"It'll give you more time." But you were adamant.
He had no answer to your strength. You didn't
want to lose your hair, be sick as a dog,
and all for the sake of a few more weeks.

It was me now who asked the cretinous
questions. It just couldn't be as hopeless
as that. Like a floundering man in a sea
of sharks, there had to be some 'get out clause'.

"But people recover who've been given
no hope. I read about a woman last week."
He gave a sympathetic shrug. Later I thought,
he would have failed if he'd given false hope.

I was in pieces and couldn't believe how well
you took it. "I would have cried had it been me."
"No you wouldn't," and you pulled me
towards you, your eyes full of love.

You'd not go down fighting.
"There's nothing to fight." But you'd make
the most of the time you had left.
"I'll go out in style and smile to the end."

You decided that you'd tell our friends.
It heartened you to see how much
So many cared. Everyone hugged you,
and all of them cried, including the men.

Have a good holiday, someone said. A cruise,
perhaps. Somewhere that's romantic, exotic.
Somewhere in the tropics. Hot. "Capricorn,"
you said and smiled, "not the other one."

Her Answer

Because you make up nicknames for my friends
  which are amusing
  and only mildly insulting;
Because you always snog me
  on the way home from the pub,
  put your hand down my knickers
  and fetch me off;
Because you bought a mirror globe
  and had me dance naked with you
  to *Stardust*;
Because we once went to the seaside
  and you bought me a kite;
Because you throw and catch a frisbee
  with such obvious glee;
Because you sing along with me in the kitchen
  using a spatula as a mic;
Because you took me to the football
  and didn't complain once when I talked
  about which player had the nicest legs;
Because you don't get too upset when they lose,
  though you took it hard when Cantona
  hung up his boots, and I sometimes
  think you care more for them
  than you do for me;
Because you cry when listening to *Nimrod*
  and *O Mio Babbino Caro*:
Because you cry when the steam clears
  at the end of *The Railway Children*;
Because you can read Tennyson like an angel;
Because you can do a stir-fry to die for;
Because I can sing *Nobody Does it Better* to you
  and mean every word.

But the question should have been:
  Why have you stayed with me?

Her Story: No Fairy Tale

Once there was a princess beautiful and fair
of face, with long blonde tresses,
shapely legs that went forever up
and breasts like two melons in a bag.

Many a suitor paid her call.
None suited her, though some had wads,
were babelicious, and a couple
well-endowed with princely pads.

For a jester was her only love.
He made her laugh, had a wiser head
than the silk shirt boys, and knew
how to do it for her in bed.

They married on a winter's day,
got filled to the brim with sex and champagne,
went back to her castle: a third floor flat
with a decent view and a welcome mat.

Now all was well for a number of years
till the princess was stricken by a terrible pain.
She sought the wise-woman in her lair,
a middle-aged woman with greying hair.

The wise-woman told her of a calamitous curse,
and said there was worse: for the man
she'd married for better or worse
would have his share of the terrible curse.

Now when she surveyed her barren lands,
she thought of her husband whom she loved.
He, too, would never see his seeds
grow tall and ripen in the sun. She became

depressed, so to cheer herself she cast a spell.
She metamorphosed into a mayfly
and offered herself to a friendly spider,
who wriggled and wriggled and wriggled inside her.

She half expected her man to leave, but he didn't, so she
transformed once more and became Queen Bee.
And many succumbed to her honey trap,
and many a drone worked hard to please.

Yet still he could not be stung to leave,
and I cannot say it made her grieve.
for she was well into her role of Queen Bee
she loved the attention, the thrill. You see,

it cast its own spell and drew her within.
And if she had any regrets or doubts,
she told herself that the others were none;
her husband was still her Number One.

But Fate never stays his hand too long,
for he cannot abide to see us safe,
and he sent to the princess a hideous crab
with clasping, poisonous pincers of death.

The wizards conferred and said it was bad,
they scratched their heads and looked quite sad.
But the princess, resigned, was more upbeat
and determined to enjoy herself.

It hadn't, she felt, been too bad an innings.
She'd had her share of fun and laughter.
Life, she said, was no fairy tale,
and we die at some point ever after.

Carnation

The blue and gold had melted away
the night-time black.
With your hand in mine we knelt
to gaze upon the first carnation
of our turmoiled year. I'm sure
you felt as I, this bud had held
its beauty so tightly to itself, held it
for this moment, for the two of us.

I recalled how you had squeezed my hand
so tightly some days before, and how
you had once said, "Wanting is lust,
needing is love," – getting to the essence
and the heart. You could have taught
those ancient Greeks a thing or two.

And now it was this perfect flower:
white upon white upon white,
the tips tinged with an almost purple
pink, and the green of the stem.
You'd once said, "It should be a colour –
carnation green. It would be in every
paint box, if I had my way."

A single globe of dew had pearled
the purple pink and caught the sun.
I pulled you to me so you could see.
You balanced yourself with an arm
around my back, and our heads touched
gently, gently.

"Will you write a poem for me
when I'm gone?" you said.
"At the end of days, when the universe
cries in pain and ends in flames,
the echo that remains will be my love,"
I said. I'd thought of it the night before.
I immediately thought how corny,
how twee it now sounds. You squeezed
my hand, and I knew when you turned
your head away, and by the little shiver
that you gave, that you were crying.

"That's lovely," you eventually said.
I turned my face to yours.
"It's not as good as what you once said."
"What's that?" you said.
"Wanting is lust, needing is love."

Ghosts

Opening a book, I found a hair pressed
between the pages –

like a bookmark.

It was one of yours. It had to be.
Your length, your colour. I'm sure
it would have had your smell
had I been brave enough.

I held it for a silent time. This is
a part of you, an actual part of you
I thought, then let it fall,
quite inexplicably.

This house hangs heavy on my heart.
Memories abound, surround
my everyday: a cornucopia
of bitter sweet.

And I remembered clearing out
my mother's things, and the guilt
I felt as I filled the skip with her life.

We have to let go of our past
before it becomes a ghost
that haunts us to our deaths.

I closed the book. I didn't cry.
But the gods are cruel today.

This Will be It From Now on, I Suppose

I can play a round every day on the links,
lie on the sofa, have forty winks
                in the afternoon.

No more beach holidays on the Med.
I can have beans on toast and fart in bed
                as much as I like.

I can bags the rag-top whenever I want,
play cards, or go on a Sunday dinner-time jaunt
                with my mates.

I can watch men wearing pads and white flannels,
watch programmes on the discovery channels
                about past wars.

Sometimes – I imagine – I'll get up to high-jinx,
spray myself all over with *lynx*,
                and wait for the women to pounce.

I can sit in a chair and just think
or sit at my desk and waste good ink
                on poetry.

If I Could Write You a Letter, My Love

I have cut the flowers and put them in a vase,
arranging them like a shower of gold and blue,
the way you used to do.
And when I make the bed, I place the heart
shaped pillow in the middle
like you used to do,
and prop the Fozzy Bear and Horny Devil
on the chair:
Fozzy for me, Horny Devil for you.

Yesterday I fingered the pebbles
we collected from the beaches we once trod.
The one we fetched from Cyprus,
when I swam round Aphrodite's Rock
to prove my love for you,
I held against my cheek.
I felt it, smooth and cold.

I also fingered the coffee table book.
There should always be a book, you said,
for guests to pick up.
I will change it one day.
I shall choose one from our study,
I shall choose it with great care.

Last night, I held your jewellery box.
I did not open it and take
your bracelet out
to count the charms,
each one a place where we made love,
recalled how friends could not believe
we'd done it in a monastery.

And remember how I used
to shake my head and tut
each time you bought a magnet
for the fridge from shops selling tat.
These, too, I finger now
and read the homespun wisdom

as I close the door.
As I close the door.

Starling

All is aches and pains,
worse than before.

The nights are lonely
in an empty nest.

Though the sun shines brightly,
the morning shivers with cold.

This will not do – I must summon up
my strength once more,

deny what I am become; become
more phoenix than what I am.

I must stretch and show
the fearlessness of youth,

remember the exuberance
of fledgling flight,

and I must test the air beneath
my wings once more.

For the sun that is here
gives off no warmth, no love.

Remainders

Anniversaries

VI

Remember how it used to be
when I loved you and you loved me,
and we couldn't afford, as we can tonight,
the food, the wine, the candlelight.

X

And so it's here – another year.
I watched you with the flowers my dear,
tearing off petals with your eyes,
endured their squeals and helpless cries:
he loves me .. he loves me not...
he loves me ..

Raindrops

The wind blew a sharp reminder
winter was not finished yet.
I pulled my coat together
and you squeezed my arm
as we walked along the beach.

Later it rained, and we
had tea together, you and I.
I sat and looked at you,
but you looked at the rain outside.
And so I came to watch

the rain upon the window.
Drops running into drops,
they crept into each other's arms
then ran as one
straight down the glass.

But still you watched
the rain outside.
And spring was always
too far away that year
to bud your love.

Arsy Versy

You come to bed late
and shove cold bottom
into the pit of my warm back.

It was not always so.
Once I used to love your bottom,
as hot as a fresh baked loaf.
And your bottom loved me.
It used to tumble onto the bed
it used to giggle at my touch,
would want to be naked,
free of cotton,
free of silk,
would smile as I gave it
what it wanted.

And afterwards would nestle
snugly in my groin,
sometimes wiggle and make
a little purring noise.

Now you come to bed late
and shove cold bottom
into the pit of my warm back.

Four Seasons of a Bad Year

Winter Day, Lose Tomorrow

Making sex upon the rug
as the fire burned low,
I fanned the dying embers
of our love.

Spring Roll

Oh, to be in April
now that she is here.
The table's set, the bed is made,
and I have some wine and beer.

Summer Goers, Some are Not

Sad to say
but your beliefs
got in the way
of our reliefs.

Fall Guy

You said you only wanted sex.
It was all that you were after.
We gorged. I had you on a plate
for breakfast, lunch and supper;
but then I went and fell for you,
and again I came a cropper.

IRON Press is among the country's longest established
independent literary publishers.
The press began operations in 1973 with IRON
Magazine which ran for 83 editions until 1997. Since
1975 we have also brought out a regular list of
individual collections of poetry, fiction and drama plus
various anthologies ranging from *Voices of
Conscience, Limerick Nation,
The Poetry of Perestroika, 100 Island Poems,
Cold IRON – Ghost Stories from the 21st Century* and
forthcoming, *Aliens* (fiction).

The press is one of the leading independent publishers
of haiku in the UK.
Since 2013 we have also run a biennial IRON Press
Festival round the harbour in our
native Cullercoats. The IRON OR Festival took place
in June 2019.

We are delighted to be a part of Inpress Ltd, which
was set up by Arts Council England to support
independent literary publishers.
Go to our website (www.ironpress.cc.uk)
for full details of our titles and activities.